ORDINARY
PEOPLE
CHANGE
—THE—
WORLD

I am
Anne Frank

BRAD MELTZER
illustrated by Christopher Eliopoulos

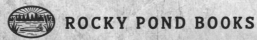
ROCKY POND BOOKS

I am ANNE FRANK.

When I was born, my sister loved laughing at my big ears.

I also had big eyes and the cutest smile.

As a girl, I loved the same things many kids love:

playing
hide-and-seek
and tag...

ice-skating...

and going to the movies.

One of the other things I really loved was writing stories.

One other thing that's important to know about me is that I'm Jewish. That's my religion.

I believe in God and in helping to make the world a better place.

But where I was born in Germany, there were people known as Nazis who didn't like those of us who were Jewish, or other groups who were different from them.

Back then, the Nazis were run by a terrible leader named Adolf Hitler who promised to make Germany strong again.

He believed that Germans were superior—and he blamed the Jews for all of Germany's problems, even though we hadn't done anything wrong.

To protect us from the Nazis, my family became refugees and moved to a city called Amsterdam, in the Netherlands.

We tried to leave the Netherlands and go to the United States, but we couldn't.

Life was good there for years—until May 10, 1940, when the Germans came to the Netherlands too. The Nazis were trying to take over the world.

When the Germans arrived in the Netherlands, they passed new laws here.

At first, Jews weren't allowed in public parks, beaches, pools, or in libraries.

Then they said we couldn't go to the movies.

Eventually, we weren't allowed to ride our own bikes, drive our own cars, or buy food at certain restaurants.

One of the worst days was when they said we had to leave our school and only be with other Jewish kids.

Every day, it seemed to get worse.

I know it sounds scary, but this isn't a story about fear.
It's a story about hope.
Even when bad things happen, there are good things all around.

Every year, my parents put all my presents out on the table.
And this year, I couldn't wait for one particular gift.

A diary.
It had its own little lock.

I started writing immediately.

Kitty was the name I gave to my diary.
   I wanted the diary to be my friend.

A few weeks later, we got terrible news.

WHAT IS IT, DEAR?

MARGOT...

OUR DAUGHTER...

THEY SENT HER A "CALL-UP" NOTICE.

We knew what a "call-up" really meant. The Nazis would send people to a concentration camp, a prison where Jews were locked up and made to work all day and night.

There was almost nothing to eat or drink. If you went there, escape was nearly impossible.

My parents were running out of options.

If we stayed, the Nazis would come for my sister.

If we tried to leave, they'd hunt us down.

My parents told us to start packing.

We could only take our most important things.

The first thing I grabbed was this diary.

A BOOK?

YES! A PLACE TO HOLD MY DAILY THOUGHTS.

We wore layers of clothes so no one would see us carrying suitcases. The hardest part was saying goodbye to my cat.

THE NEIGHBORS WILL TAKE GOOD CARE OF HER.

I PROMISE.

I LOVE YOU, MOORTJE.

As we snuck out, there were four of us— then another family of three met us there.

Our new home was about the size of a one-bedroom apartment, for seven of us.

THIS WAS MY PARENTS' LIVING ROOM AND BEDROOM.

HOW ARE WE ALL GOING TO FIT?

ATTIC

BOOKCASE ENTRANCE

AND THIS WAS FOR ME AND MY SISTER.

Upstairs was another room—it was a bedroom, kitchen, and living room all in one—for the van Pels, the other Jewish family hiding with us.

Plus there was a place for their son, Peter.

It wasn't an easy place to live.

During weekdays, we had to whisper—we could never talk in a normal voice.

All the windows were covered. And since shoes were noisy on the wood floors, we usually wore socks to be extra quiet.

SHHHH.

ONE WRONG MOVE, AND THE NAZIS MIGHT FIND US.

IT WOULD'VE BEEN EASY TO COMPLAIN,

BUT I DECIDED TO LOOK AT THE BRIGHT SIDE.

It may be damp and lopsided, but there's probably not a more comfortable hiding place in all of Amsterdam. No, in all of Holland.

To make it feel more normal, I decorated my walls with pictures of movie stars.

MY DAD SURPRISED ME BY BRINGING ALONG MY COLLECTION OF MAGAZINES.

To make everyone laugh, Peter and I would dress up. He wore his mom's dress, and I wore his suit.

TA-DAH!

There was one big bright spot, though—the non-Jewish helpers who risked their own lives to protect us.

The Nazis threatened to punish anyone who helped the Jewish people.

But these amazing people decided it was more important to do the right thing and help us.

Our hiding spot was tiny.

But when someone needs help, you can't turn away.

We hid in the Secret Annex for two years and one month.

I went to school here.

I wanted to be a famous writer—to make an impact on people's lives.

With eight of us crammed together, our world was very small.
But if you look for what's good, you'll find it.

It had the one window that wasn't covered,
where I could see the blue sky and this one
chestnut tree.

grew up here.

I saw the world from here.

Who knows, maybe our religion will teach the world and all the people in it about goodness.

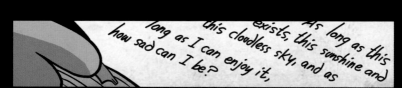

...As long as this exists, this sunshine and this cloudless sky, and as long as I can enjoy it, how sad can I be?

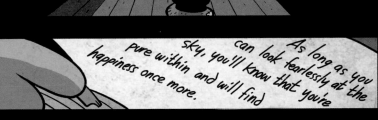

As long as you can look fearlessly at the sky, you'll know that you're pure within and will find happiness once more.

I still believe, in spite of everything, that people are truly good at heart.

And eventually, the world saw me.

In my life, there were many reasons to be sad.
And lonely.
And scared.
But there were also many reasons to love.
And laugh.
And hope.

You can always find light in the darkest places.
That's what hope is.
It's a fire within you.
You decide when to light it.
And when it burns bright…

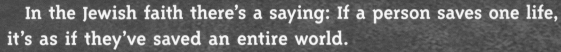

In the Jewish faith there's a saying: If a person saves one life, it's as if they've saved an entire world.

Throughout your life, you'll find people who need help.

Be a helper.

Be the one who does the right thing.

When you see something that's unfair, do not be silent.

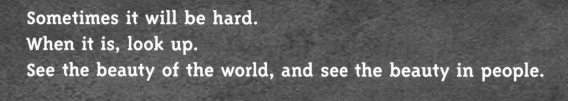

Sometimes it will be hard.
When it is, look up.
See the beauty of the world, and see the beauty in people.

Now you know my story, and I'm a part of yours.
Never forget.
The world depends on it.

I am Anne Frank, and I believe
that people are truly good at heart.

"Think of all the beauty in yourself and in everything around you and be happy."

—ANNE FRANK

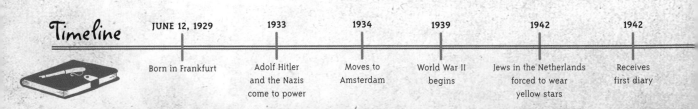

Timeline	JUNE 12, 1929	1933	1934	1939	1942	1942
	Born in Frankfurt	Adolf Hitler and the Nazis come to power	Moves to Amsterdam	World War II begins	Jews in the Netherlands forced to wear yellow stars	Receives first diary

Margot, Otto, Anne, and Edith Frank, 1941

Pages from Anne's diary

Badge that Jewish people were forced to wear

Otto Frank's office building (middle), 1947

Anne's room in the Secret Annex

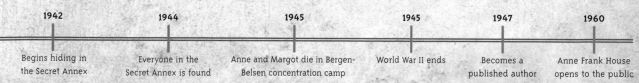

1942	1944	1945	1945	1947	1960
Begins hiding in the Secret Annex	Everyone in the Secret Annex is found	Anne and Margot die in Bergen-Belsen concentration camp	World War II ends	Becomes a published author	Anne Frank House opens to the public

*In memory of Anne Frank and the six million Jewish victims of the Holocaust,
and in honor of all the righteous helpers who risked their lives
by coming to the aid of those who needed it.*
–B.M. & C.E.

For historical accuracy, we used Anne Frank's actual words whenever possible.
For more of her true voice, we recommend and acknowledge *The Diary of a Young Girl* by Anne Frank.
Special thanks to Sharon R. Douglas and Maureen McNeil of the Anne Frank Center for Mutual Respect,
as well as Holocaust Era historian Peter Black for their input on early drafts.

SOURCES

The Diary of a Young Girl: The Definitive Edition by Anne Frank (Doubleday, 2001)
Anne Frank: The Biography by Melissa Müller (Holt, 1998)
AnneFrank.org: The Anne Frank House website and interactive tour

FURTHER READING FOR KIDS

The Tree in the Courtyard: Looking Through Anne Frank's Window by Jeff Gottesfeld (Knopf, 2016)
The Cat Who Lived with Anne Frank by David Lee Miller and Steven Jay Rubin (Philomel, 2019)
Who Was Anne Frank? by Ann Abramson (Penguin Workshop, 2007)
What Was the Holocaust? by Gail Herman (Penguin Workshop, 2019)

ROCKY POND BOOKS
An imprint of Penguin Random House LLC, New York

First published in the United States of America by Dial Books for Young Readers, an imprint of Penguin Random House LLC, 2020
This edition published by Rocky Pond Books, an imprint of Penguin Random House LLC, 2023

Text copyright © 2020 by Forty-four Steps, Inc. • Illustrations copyright © 2020 by Christopher Eliopoulos
Pages 38–39: Photos of Anne at her desk, the Frank family, and the bedroom (photo by Allard Bovenberg) courtesy of the Anne Frank House, Amsterdam.
Photo of Anne's diary pages courtesy of Anne Frank Fonds Basel/Getty Images. Photo of the Star of David courtesy of the United States Holocaust Memorial Museum Collection,
Gift of Sig Feiger. Photo of Otto Frank's office building by Carel Blazer courtesy of MAI/Amsterdam.

Rocky Pond Books is a registered trademark and the colophon is a trademark of Penguin Random House LLC.
The Penguin colophon is a registered trademark of Penguin Books Limited.

Visit us online at PenguinRandomHouse.com.

LIBRARY OF CONGRESS CATALOGING-IN-PUBLICATION DATA IS AVAILABLE.

Manufactured in China on acid-free paper

ISBN 9780525555940 • 10 9 8 7 6 5

Designed by Jason Henry • Text set in Triplex • The artwork for this book was created digitally.

This is a work of nonfiction. Some names and identifying details have been changed.

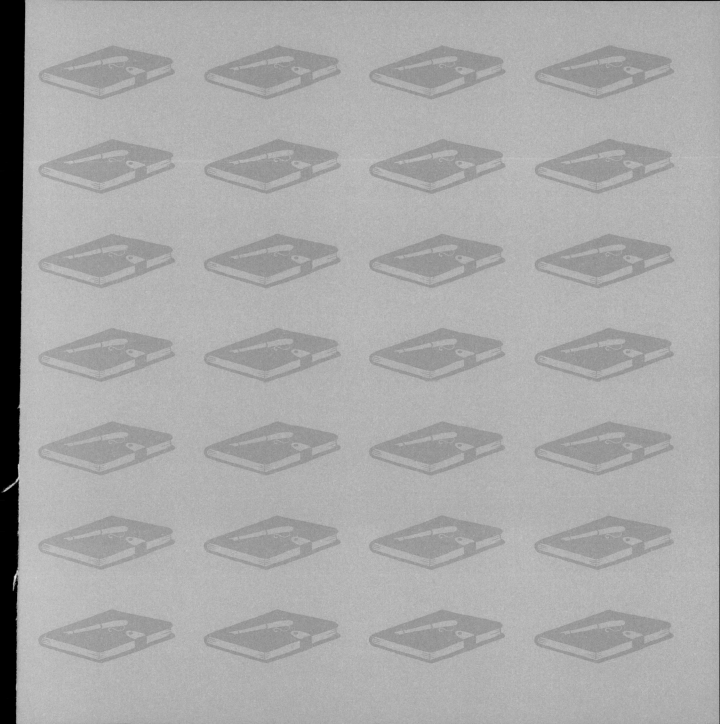

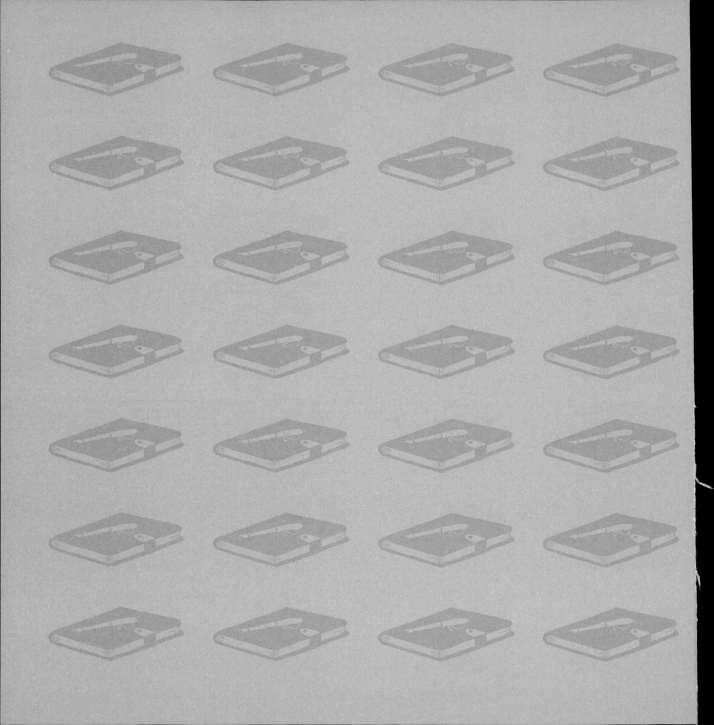